TEMPLE CITY~

KANCHEEPURAM

Published By

www.poetryworld.org

Temple City - Kancheepuram
Written by D. Varsha
Published by: Poetry World Org.
Publisher's Address: Haryana
Printed under PWO in India

 Special credits to Aksha Ratnesh, Dr.Niveditha and Dr.Nitin Chopra.

Edition: I (2025)
ISBN (Paperback) - 9789367237311
Book Design by POETRY WORLD

TEMPLE CITY~

KANCHEEPURAM

D. VARSHA

TEMPLE CITY - KANCHEEPURAM

Kancheepuram — a city where every stone tells a story, every temple whispers of divinity, and time itself pauses in reverence.

Temple City - Kancheepuram is a lyrical journey through one of South India's most sacred and architecturally resplendent cities. From the soaring gopurams of Ekambareswarar to the serene sandstone carvings of Kailasanathar, this book weaves together history, art, mythology, and devotion. Through vivid descriptions, rare insights, and cultural depth, it brings to life the living heritage of a city once hailed as the "Spiritual Capital of South India."

Whether you are a seeker of beauty, a student of history, or a pilgrim at heart, this book invites you to walk the timeless corridors of Kancheepuram — where stone breathes, and the sacred endures.

D. VARSHA

D. Varsha, daughter of S. Dhanraj and D. Sundari, is a bright and imaginative student from Class 8. Born on October 5, 2012, Varsha is a creative young mind with a deep curiosity for culture, color, and history. Her favorite colors – red, blue, and black – reflect the vibrant layers of her personality.

She shares a special bond with her loving sibling, D. Kanishka, who is her constant support and source of strength. Varsha's heart is full of affection for dogs, her favorite animals, and she treasures her close friendship with Lak Suruthi. Her beloved aunties, Jasmine Crena and Yamini, hold an inspiring place in her life, encouraging her with their warmth and wisdom.

She is also deeply grateful to her favorite teachers, Asha Mam and Hema Mam, whose guidance has helped shape her learning journey. With a budding interest in global cultures and powerhouses of history, her favorite centuries are India and Russia.

With her debut work "Temple City - Kancheepuram", Varsha brings to life the sacred beauty of ancient temples through the eyes of a young dreamer – capturing the heart of a city carved in stone and faith.

FOREWORD

Kanchipuram, a city where history and heritage are intricately woven into the fabric of its existence, stands as a testament to the enduring legacy of Tamil civilization. Known as the "City of a Thousand Temples," it is a place where the divine and the earthly exist in harmony, where the echoes of ancient prayers and the weight of centuries-old stone carvings continue to resonate in every corner.

This book seeks to unravel the essence of Kanchipuram, not merely as a geographical location, but as a living, breathing symbol of spirituality, artistry, and cultural continuity. From the towering grandeur of its temples to the delicate intricacies of its silk sarees, Kanchipuram is a canvas of divine craftsmanship, historical milestones, and architectural marvels. It is a city that has, for millennia, stood at the crossroads of great dynasties, kingdoms, and religions, and yet, it has preserved its distinct identity in the face of time's inevitable passage.

The significance of Kanchipuram transcends its temples and silk; it is the embodiment of an unbroken cultural thread that binds generations, a source of inspiration for poets, artists, philosophers, and devout followers alike. Here, the timeless rhythms of devotion have been passed from the Nayanmars and Alvars to the modern-day devotees, shaping the spiritual landscape of Tamil Nadu and the larger Indian subcontinent.

As you journey through these pages, you will come to understand not only the grandeur of Kanchipuram's architecture but also the profound connection between its rivers, its people, and the land itself. The book invites you to immerse yourself in a world where faith and tradition have weathered the ages, where every stone speaks a story, and where the very air is thick with history.

It is with great reverence for the past and an eye towards the future that this narrative is presented, offering a glimpse into a city that, though steeped in ancient tradition, continues to inspire and shape the present. May this work serve as a humble tribute to Kanchipuram, a place that remains, in the hearts of many, a beacon of culture, devotion, and eternal grace.

D Varsha

ACKNOWLEDGEMENTS

With deep gratitude and love, I dedicate this work to those who have shaped my journey with their unwavering support, encouragement, and inspiration.

To my beloved parents, Mr Dhanraj and Mrs Thiripurusundari thank you for being my first teachers and my greatest supporters. Your sacrifices and prayers have been the foundation of all my achievements.

To my dear sister Kanishka, your love and laughter are a constant source of joy in my life.

To my cherished grandparents, Grandfather Ramu and Grandmother Jaya, your wisdom and blessings have guided me every step of the way.

To my close friend Lak Suruthi, thank you for standing by me with loyalty and affection.

To my loving aunty Dr. Jasmine Crena, your grace and encouragement have inspired me more than words can say.

To Aunty Yamini and Aunty Rajamani, your kindness and presence have been a source of comfort and strength.

To Asha Mam and Hema Mam, thank you for your mentorship and gentle guidance.

To my dear relatives – Aunty Shayamala, Muthulakshmi, Dhamlakshmi, and Amuthavalli – your support has been invaluable.

To Mr. Kannan, thank you for your assistance and thoughtful encouragement.

To Uncle Ravi and Uncle Balaji, your presence in my life has been a blessing.

To Mr. Lakshminarayanan Uncle, a truly kind soul – thank you for your silent strength and warmth.

To Mr Shanmugam and Kaniyamal, thank you for being part of my journey with your affection and support.

A heartfelt thank you to Creative Writers for this wonderful opportunity – your platform has been a stepping stone in bringing my vision to life.

Each of you has touched my life in a special way. This book is a reflection of all your love and blessings.

INDEX

CHAPTER 1:

GEOGRAPHY AND MYTHOS

Located approximately 75 kilometers southwest of Chennai in the state of Tamil Nadu, Kanchipuram rests along the sacred banks of the Vegavati River, a modest yet hallowed tributary of the Palar. Though its terrain may seem unassuming to the casual eye, the city is steeped in a spiritual geography that transcends mere topography. In both Tamil and Sanskrit traditions, Kanchipuram is celebrated not only for its antiquity but for its divine resonance. It is one of the *Sapta Moksha-puris*—the seven sacred cities of India believed to grant *moksha,* or liberation from the cycle of birth and death. Alongside cities like Varanasi and Ujjain, Kanchipuram is revered as a threshold between the temporal and the timeless.

Myths cluster around its soil like morning mist upon its groves. It is said that sages such as Vyasa, Patanjali, and Agastya once wandered here, meditating beneath venerable trees that still whisper their prayers into the wind. The city's temples—each a cosmic diagram rendered in stone—are believed to be dwelling places not only of gods but of celestial energies that converge and radiate outward. Lord Shiva, as Ekambareswarar, is said to have created a lingam out of sand beneath a mango tree on the banks of the Vegavati, praying for Parvati's hand. Lord Vishnu, as Varadaraja Perumal, is said to have risen from the waters of the temple tank to bless his devotees.

The rivers of Kanchipuram carry more than water—they carry memory and myth. The Vegavati herself is considered a purifier, her flow sanctified by the prayers and rituals offered on her banks for millennia. But more mystically, the subterranean Sarasvati—the fabled lost river of the Vedas—is believed by many to run beneath the surface, unseen but spiritually potent. Tradition holds that at certain rare confluences, the hidden Sarasvati meets the visible Vegavati in a confluence of grace, bathing the land in unseen blessings and purifying even the most stubborn karmic residue.

Thus, the geography of Kanchipuram is inseparable from its mythos. It is not merely a city of temples; it is itself a temple writ large, each street a *pradakshina* path, each riverbank a sanctum. Here, the stone becomes scripture, and the air is thick with the chanting of unseen sages. To walk its roads is to tread upon the border of two realms—the earthly and the eternal, the material and the metaphysical. Kanchipuram does not simply exist in time; it breathes with the rhythm of myth, a city where every breeze recalls a benediction.

Rivers of Reverence: The Sacred Waters of Kanchipuram

Though Kanchipuram lies inland, far from the confluence of great river systems like the Ganga or the Cauvery, its spiritual identity is deeply entwined with water. The rivers that flow through and beneath its soil are not measured merely in cubic meters but in verses, visions, and veneration. Each stream and subterranean current is charged with a sacredness that elevates the city beyond the ordinary plane of geography.

Foremost among these is the **Vegavati River**, a tributary of the larger **Palar River**, which courses through northern Tamil Nadu. Though the Vegavati may appear as a seasonal stream—gentle and almost reticent in its flow—its significance is anything but modest. The river skirts the city like a silver girdle, encircling many of its ancient temples and sacred sites. It is here, on the banks of the Vegavati, that Lord Shiva, in his manifestation as **Ekambareswarar**, is believed to have fashioned a lingam from the river's sand under the sacred mango tree (*sthala vriksha*), praying for reunion with Parvati. During the monsoons, when the river swells and murmurs with ancient song, devotees believe its waters are especially potent for ritual purification.

The **Palar River**, into which the Vegavati ultimately flows, serves as the broader lifeline of this region. Though its flow has diminished over time due to shifting rain patterns and human intervention, it remains symbolically vital. In local tradition, the Palar is often imagined not just as a geographical presence but as a witness—an ancient entity that has watched dynasties rise and fall, temples rise from the earth, and prayers rise from lips worn with longing.

Yet perhaps most mystical of all is the **invisible Sarasvati**—the legendary river of the Vedic age, said to have vanished from earthly sight but never from spiritual consciousness. According to certain streams of tradition, especially among temple priests and mystics, the Sarasvati flows beneath Kanchipuram's soil, unseen but ever-present. In this view, Kanchipuram is more than a sacred site; it is a *tirtha,* a crossing place where the hidden river of divine wisdom meets the earthly flow of mortal devotion. The Sarasvati is said to unite with the Vegavati at secret confluences known only to the gods and the spiritually attuned, imbuing the land with an aura of enlightenment and quiet mysticism.

This triadic network—Vegavati, Palar, and the subterranean Sarasvati—forms the sacred hydrography of Kanchipuram. They are not merely watercourses but carriers of *tapas* (spiritual heat), *bhakti* (devotion), and *jnana* (wisdom). Even the city's numerous temple tanks, such as the *Ananta*

Saras, Chakra Tirtha, and *Kampa Nadi,* are considered sacred extensions of these rivers, connected through unseen veins of spiritual water. Bathing in them during festivals like **Maha Shivaratri** or **Vaikunta Ekadasi** is believed to wash away sins and bestow divine merit.

In the worldview of Kanchipuram, rivers do not merely irrigate crops—they irrigate the soul. They are living, breathing presences, flowing with stories as much as with silt, bearing forward the prayers of a thousand generations. To sit on their banks, to hear the lapping of their waters, is to enter a deeper listening—to attune oneself to the murmur of myth, the rhythm of ritual, and the silence that lies beneath both.

CHAPTER 2:

DYNASTIES OF KANCHIPURAM: THRONES BENEATH TEMPLE SPIRES

Kanchipuram, the "City of a Thousand Temples," has for centuries stood not only as a bastion of faith but also as a crucible of kingship. Its stones whisper the names of monarchs who walked its streets, raised its sanctuaries, and wove its destiny into the grand tapestry of South Indian civilization. Across centuries, it was courted and claimed by a succession of dynasties, each leaving its own imprimatur on the city's temples, language, art, and faith.

The Early Tamil Kingdoms: Sangam Echoes

Though Kanchipuram's most documented royal past begins with the Pallavas, references to the city date back even earlier, to the Sangam age (circa 3rd century BCE–3rd century CE), when it was part of the **Thondai Nadu** region. Ancient Tamil literature such as the *Perumpāṇāṟṟuppaṭai* sings of Kanchipuram as a prosperous settlement, famed for its fine cloth, learned scholars, and flourishing markets. It was ruled by early **Velir chieftains** and was already emerging as a cultural nucleus where Jainism, Buddhism, and the early Tamil forms of Shaivism and Vaishnavism mingled.

The Pallavas: Architects of Eternal Stone

It is with the rise of the **Pallava dynasty** (circa 4th–9th century CE) that Kanchipuram truly began its transformation from a flourishing town to a radiant royal capital. The Pallavas, whose origins are still debated by historians, were the first major rulers to establish Kanchipuram as their capital, elevating it to the status of an imperial and spiritual seat.

Under kings such as **Simhavishnu**, **Mahendravarman I**, and especially **Narasimhavarman I (Mamallan)**, the Pallavas not only defended their realm from northern incursions but also became legendary patrons of architecture, literature, and religion. They pioneered South Indian rock-cut and structural temple architecture, with nearby **Mahabalipuram (Mamallapuram)** serving as an artistic outpost of their vision.

In Kanchipuram itself, they built monumental temples such as the **Kailasanathar Temple**, a stone symphony dedicated to Lord Shiva, and supported both **Shaiva** and **Vaishnava** traditions. The city under Pallava rule was a crossroads of learning, where Sanskrit and Tamil flourished side by side. Chinese traveler **Xuanzang (Hiuen Tsang)**, who visited in the 7th century CE, described Kanchipuram as a great center of Buddhist learning, housing thousands of monks and monasteries—an echo of its religious plurality.

The Cholas: Temple-Builders and Empire-Weavers

With the waning of the Pallavas, the **Chola dynasty** rose to prominence, eventually incorporating Kanchipuram into their ever-expanding empire by the 10th century CE. Though **Thanjavur** remained the Chola capital, Kanchipuram retained its importance as a sacred city and administrative hub.

The Cholas enriched Kanchipuram's temple complexes, adding inscriptions, gilded towers (*vimanas*), and land grants for temple maintenance. Great rulers such as **Rajaraja Chola I** and **Rajendra Chola I** patronized the city's Shaiva temples and built richly endowed mathas and agraharams for Vedic scholars.

The Chola inscriptions in temples like **Ekambareswarar** and **Kamakshi Amman** are a historian's goldmine—detailing not only religious endowments but also records of economic life, taxation, irrigation, and caste structures. Under the Cholas, Kanchipuram was a node in a vast oceanic network of Tamil trade and cultural exchange, stretching from Southeast Asia to Sri Lanka.

The Later Pandyas and the Interregnum

After the Cholas, the **Pandyas** and their successors briefly controlled Kanchipuram, particularly in the 13th century. These decades were marked by dynastic conflict and shifting alliances, with the city occasionally falling into the hands of local feudatories and minor powers. Nevertheless, temple rituals and intellectual life continued, sustained by hereditary priestly lineages and land grants.

The Vijayanagara Empire: Renaissance of Devotion

The 14th century saw the resurgence of South Indian power under the **Vijayanagara Empire**, which came to dominate Kanchipuram and Tamil Nadu in the face of northern invasions. Under emperors like **Krishnadevaraya** and **Achyuta Deva Raya**, Kanchipuram witnessed a remarkable spiritual and architectural revival.

The Vijayanagara rulers, deeply committed to Hindu orthodoxy and temple culture, renovated and expanded many of the city's great temples. The soaring **gopurams (gateway towers)** of **Varadaraja Perumal**, **Ekambareswarar**, and **Kamakshi Amman** bear the unmistakable stamp of Vijayanagara architecture—tall, ornamented towers filled with stucco sculptures of gods, demons, and dancers.

It was during this time that Kanchipuram emerged as a stronghold of **Sri Vaishnavism**, especially under the influence of theologians like **Vedanta Desika**, and the city became one of the principal sites of **Pancha Kanchis**, centers of spiritual authority and learning.

The Nayaks and Nawabs: Fracture and Faith

After the decline of Vijayanagara in the 17th century, power devolved into the hands of the **Nayaks of Gingee** and **Thanjavur**, and later the **Nawabs of the Carnatic**. The city became a contested territory during the **Carnatic Wars** of the 18th century, caught between the ambitions of the French, the British, and regional powers.

Though political turbulence abounded, Kanchipuram's spiritual institutions remained resilient. Temple worship continued with patronage from local chieftains and communities, and the city retained its reputation as a place of pilgrimage and Sanskritic learning.

The Colonial Period and Beyond

Under **British colonial rule**, Kanchipuram became part of the Madras Presidency, and while its political significance waned, its cultural and religious identity remained intact. In the 19th and early 20th centuries, the city saw a resurgence of interest in traditional scholarship, led by figures such as **Chandrashekarendra Saraswati**, the revered Shankaracharya of the **Kanchi Kamakoti Peetham**, who made the city his seat and revitalized Advaita Vedanta in the region.

Legacy of Rule, Continuity of Faith

The dynasties that ruled Kanchipuram may have faded into the dust of history, but their legacy is etched into the city's temples, rituals, manuscripts, and collective memory. Pallava pillars, Chola inscriptions, Vijayanagara towers—each is a fragment of a civilizational mosaic where temporal power served an eternal purpose. Here, the scepter and the sanctum coexisted, and kings became devotees beneath the same spires they raised.

Kanchipuram today stands not just as a repository of political history, but as a city where dynasties became dharma, and rule gave way to reverence.

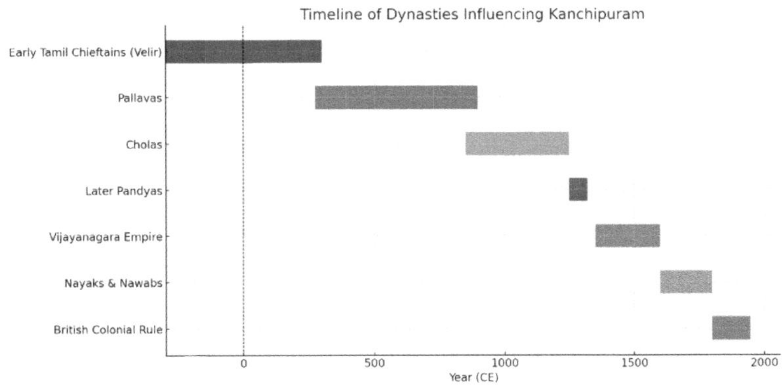

Image Reference - open access sources from internet

CHAPTER 3:

TEMPLES OF LIGHT AND SHADOW: SACRED GEOMETRY AND ETERNAL FLAME

Kanchipuram is not merely a city; it is a mandala carved in stone, a hymnal of granite where every temple sings a different note of the same divine melody. Here, temples are not passive relics but living entities—breathing sanctuaries of devotion, guardians of memory, and mirrors of cosmic design. They are both luminous and mysterious, radiant and austere—temples of light and shadow.

The phrase is no mere metaphor. In Kanchipuram's temples, light and shadow dance with divine intent. As the sun arcs across the sky, its rays are caught, filtered, and redirected by the towering *gopurams,* latticed corridors, and sanctum niches—creating shifting tapestries of gold and gloom. Illumination is not constant; it is revealed, like grace, in moments. The temples are designed so that even a shaft of light falling upon the deity at a certain hour feels like a visitation from the eternal.

Ekambareswarar Temple: Light of the Earth

Dedicated to Lord Shiva, the **Ekambareswarar Temple** is a vast sprawl of devotion and design, one of the largest in South India. Here, the element of **earth** is sacralized. The presiding lingam is said to have been formed by Parvati herself from the sands of the Vegavati River, and sheltered by a mango tree beneath which Shiva performed penance.

As light filters through the stone corridors of this temple, it falls in slanting shafts, illuminating only portions of the deity or the sanctum wall—reminding the seeker that the full truth is never seen at once. The interplay of architectural shadow and spiritual yearning mirrors the devotee's own pilgrimage—from ignorance to partial understanding to the fleeting blaze of insight.

Kamakshi Amman Temple: The Flame of Compassion

If Ekambareswarar grounds the city in ascetic fire, the **Kamakshi Amman Temple** bathes it in maternal warmth. Here, the goddess sits alone—unlike other forms of Shakti who are seen with consorts—seated in deep yogic stillness upon a Sri Chakra. She is the embodiment of *Gnana Shakti*, the power of wisdom, and her golden visage is both blinding and serene.

Within this temple, the shadow becomes a sanctifier. The sanctum is dim, lit by the trembling flames of oil lamps that flicker like thoughts in meditation. The darkness here is not the absence of light, but its containment—a womb of silence and stillness, where the devotee is cradled in the unspoken. Pilgrims often emerge not with jubilance, but with tears—the kind born not of sorrow, but of recognition.

Varadaraja Perumal Temple: The Glory that Rises

Among the greatest Vishnu temples in South India, the **Varadaraja Perumal Temple** rises on the banks of the Kampa River, its sprawling complex echoing Vaishnavite chants and philosophical discourses. The presiding deity, Lord Varadaraja, is venerated not only by devotees but also by scholars, for this temple was a bastion of the **Sri Vaishnava tradition** and the teachings of **Ramanuja** and **Vedanta Desika**.

Light plays a ceremonial role here. Once every forty years, the deity's original wooden idol—**Atthi Varadar**—is raised from beneath the temple tank and brought out for public *darshan*. The act itself is an allegory of hidden divinity rising into vision—just as the truth of existence is submerged until lifted by devotion.

Within the temple's inner sanctum, lanterns light up the deep, incense-dark halls with solemn reverence. Even the most elaborate sculptural friezes—celestial elephants, chariots, dancers—emerge only as shadows on stone until touched by fire or dawn. One sees, quite literally, "through a glass darkly," until grace lifts the veil.

Kailasanathar Temple: Sculpted Silence

Standing as a jewel of Pallava architecture, the **Kailasanathar Temple** is smaller in scale but monumental in spirit. Built by **Rajasimha Pallava**, this 8th-century Shiva temple is more of a poem than a structure. Its sandstone carvings are minutely detailed, narrating tales of cosmic dance, divine battles, and meditative repose.

Here, the shadow itself seems curated. Narrow passageways encircle the sanctum, where devotees must crawl or stoop—a symbolic journey through darkness and constraint, leading to the light of the central deity. Pilgrims emerge transformed, having symbolically passed through the birth canal of spiritual rebirth.

Temples as Cosmograph

The temples of Kanchipuram are not random constructions but deliberate **cosmographs**—spatial diagrams of the universe. The central sanctum (*garbhagriha*) is the axis mundi, the navel of the world, where the divine dwells in concentrated presence. From there, concentric layers of halls and corridors extend outward like ripples in time and consciousness.

Light, in this schema, is not incidental but theological. It pierces the darkness as insight pierces doubt. The *pradakshina*(circumambulation) path is often walked in low light, evoking the seeker's slow progress around the truth, never quite reaching the center without humility.

Light and Shadow as Devotional Language

In these temples, light and shadow are not opposites but companions. The flickering of a lamp, the fall of twilight upon a sculpted face, the sun striking the *vimana* at solstice—all become modes of divine communication. Day and night, stone and flame, silence and chant—these binary forces do not conflict, but coalesce.

The devotee's own inner world mirrors this architecture. For every revelation, a concealment; for every divine encounter, a period of waiting in the dark. The temple teaches not by sermon but by structure. It says: walk, wait, watch. Light will find you. Until then, let the shadow teach you stillness.

Architectural Features: Pillars of the Sacred Cosmos

The temples of Kanchipuram are not merely places of prayer—they are sacred instruments, precisely tuned to invoke the divine across stone and time. Their architectural features are not decorative afterthoughts but metaphysical utterances, each element a syllable in a liturgy of space. The *gopuram*, the *vimana*, the *mandapa*, the *prakara*, and the *tirtha*—together they shape a living cosmos in stone, guiding the devotee from the periphery of the mundane to the blazing stillness of the sanctum within.

Gopuram: The Gateway as Threshold

Towering above city streets and temple walls, the **gopuram** is the first to greet the eye—and yet, it is not an end, but a beginning. Literally meaning "king's gateway" (*go* - cow/earth, *puram* - town/gate), the gopuram is the threshold between the temporal and the eternal.

In Kanchipuram, especially during the Vijayanagara and later Nayaka periods, the gopurams soared ever higher, adorned with profuse stucco sculptures of gods, demons, celestial dancers, and mythical beasts. They serve as spiritual mountains, visual metaphors for ascent, and pedagogical tools—entire epics carved in tiers for the eyes of pilgrims. Whether it is the east gopuram of **Ekambareswarar** or the towering gateway of **Varadaraja Perumal**, each is a cosmic ascent, a visual ladder to the divine.

At dawn, light touches the highest reaches of the gopuram first—just as divine truth often first appears in its most elevated forms.

Vimana: The Axis of Ascent

While the gopuram beckons from afar, it is the **vimana**—the tower above the sanctum—that crowns the heart of the temple. Unlike the gopuram, the vimana is inward-facing, more compact, and always placed directly above the **garbhagriha**, the womb-chamber of the deity.

In Kanchipuram, the vimanas are architectural epiphanies. The sandstone *shikhara* of **Kailasanathar Temple**, with its lotus-bud finial, is a Pallava-era gem—restrained, symmetrical, and radiant with symbolic resonance. In contrast, the gold-plated vimana of **Varadaraja Perumal** sparkles like Surya's chariot, signifying Vishnu's sovereign stillness at the center of all motion.

The vimana is the symbolic **Meru**, the cosmic mountain, and just as the mountain's peak meets the sky, the vimana touches the heavens—uniting the human with the transcendent.

Mandapa: The Hall of Gathering and Grace

Between the gateway and the sanctum lies the **mandapa**—the pillared hall that holds together ritual, rhythm, and community. These spaces, often open on all sides, are where devotees wait, chant, meditate, or witness the rituals and festivals that animate the temple calendar.

Kanchipuram's temples feature a variety of mandapas—*ardha mandapas* (anterooms), *maha mandapas* (great halls), and *Kalyana mandapas* (wedding halls). The 100-pillared mandapa of **Varadaraja Perumal Temple** is an ocean of stone, each pillar a world of carvings: horses frozen mid-gallop, warriors in combat, gods in graceful repose. These are not merely supports for the roof; they are narrative scrolls, theological commentaries, and silent congregants of every prayer.

During processions, it is in the mandapa that the deity halts, allowing the light of lamps and the murmur of hymns to merge with the silence of stone.

Temple Tanks (Tirthas): Waters that Remember

No temple in Kanchipuram is complete without its **tirtha**—a sacred tank, often vast, bordered by steps and stories. These waters are not ornamental; they are elemental, sanctified through time and myth. Pilgrims bathe here not to cleanse the body, but to unburden the soul.

Each tank has a name, a legend, and a rhythm:

- The **Anaikatta Kulam** near Ekambareswarar is said to have been created by Shiva himself.

- The **Pushkarni** of Varadaraja Temple hides the wooden idol of **Atthi Varadar**, submerged for decades before his resurrection in ritual.

- The **Chakra Tirtha**, associated with Vishnu's discus, is believed to be a site of absolution.

At dawn, the tanks mirror the sky; at twilight, they hold shadows of spires. They are the reflecting pools of the soul—where gods appear not in form, but in ripple and reflection.

Prakara and Circumambulation: Sacred Geometry in Motion

The **prakara**, or enclosed pathway around the sanctum, is where the devotee walks in slow, measured steps. This act of **pradakshina**—

circumambulation—is not merely physical but symbolic: a walking meditation that enacts the orbit of the self around the divine center.

Many temples in Kanchipuram have multiple *prakaras,* encircling the deity like cosmic shells. The inner walls are often lined with bronze processional icons (*utsava murthis*), stories in bas-relief, and niches that house guardian deities and saints. Moving from outer prakara to inner sanctum is thus both a spatial and spiritual contraction—a journey inward.

The Temple as Cosmos, the Devotee as Pilgrim-Star

In sum, the architectural features of Kanchipuram's temples are not simply feats of engineering, but articulations of a worldview. They embody a metaphysical cartography where every stone is placed with purpose, every dimension echoes scriptural proportions, and every angle is an invitation to inner alignment.

In this sacred city, architecture is not inert. It breathes, listens, instructs. A gopuram rises like a question, a vimana resolves like a mantra. A mandapa receives the world, a tirtha returns it purified. And in the heart of it all, in the sanctum dimly lit, sits the formless made form—awaiting the devotee whose journey through light and shadow ends not in sight, but in silence.

Architectural Features: Pillars of the Sacred Cosmos

The temples of Kanchipuram are not merely places of prayer—they are sacred instruments, precisely tuned to invoke the divine across stone and time. Their architectural features are not decorative afterthoughts but metaphysical utterances, each element a syllable in a liturgy of space. The *gopuram,* the *vimana,* the *mandapa,* the *prakara,* and the *tirtha*—together they shape a living cosmos in stone, guiding the devotee from the periphery of the mundane to the blazing stillness of the sanctum within.

Gopuram: The Gateway as Threshold

Towering above city streets and temple walls, the **gopuram** is the first to greet the eye—and yet, it is not an end, but a beginning. Literally meaning "king's gateway" (*go* - cow/earth, *puram* - town/gate), the gopuram is the threshold between the temporal and the eternal.

In Kanchipuram, especially during the Vijayanagara and later Nayaka periods, the gopurams soared ever higher, adorned with profuse stucco sculptures of gods, demons, celestial dancers, and mythical beasts. They serve as spiritual mountains, visual metaphors for ascent, and pedagogical tools—entire epics carved in tiers for the eyes of pilgrims. Whether it is the east gopuram of **Ekambareswarar** or the towering gateway of **Varadaraja Perumal**, each is a cosmic ascent, a visual ladder to the divine.

At dawn, light touches the highest reaches of the gopuram first—just as divine truth often first appears in its most elevated forms.

Vimana: The Axis of Ascent

While the gopuram beckons from afar, it is the **vimana**—the tower above the sanctum—that crowns the heart of the temple. Unlike the gopuram, the vimana is inward-facing, more compact, and always placed directly above the **garbhagriha**, the womb-chamber of the deity.

In Kanchipuram, the vimanas are architectural epiphanies. The sandstone *shikhara* of **Kailasanathar Temple**, with its lotus-bud finial, is a Pallava-era gem—restrained, symmetrical, and radiant with symbolic resonance. In contrast, the gold-plated vimana of **Varadaraja Perumal** sparkles like Surya's chariot, signifying Vishnu's sovereign stillness at the center of all motion.

The vimana is the symbolic **Meru**, the cosmic mountain, and just as the mountain's peak meets the sky, the vimana touches the heavens—uniting the human with the transcendent.

Mandapa: The Hall of Gathering and Grace

Between the gateway and the sanctum lies the **mandapa**—the pillared hall that holds together ritual, rhythm, and community. These spaces, often open on all sides, are where devotees wait, chant, meditate, or witness the rituals and festivals that animate the temple calendar.

Kanchipuram's temples feature a variety of mandapas—*ardha mandapas* (anterooms), *maha mandapas* (great halls), and *Kalyana mandapas* (wedding halls). The 100-pillared mandapa of **Varadaraja Perumal Temple** is an ocean of stone, each pillar a world of carvings: horses frozen mid-gallop, warriors in combat, gods in graceful repose. These are not merely supports for the roof; they are narrative scrolls, theological commentaries, and silent congregants of every prayer.

During processions, it is in the mandapa that the deity halts, allowing the light of lamps and the murmur of hymns to merge with the silence of stone.

Temple Tanks (Tirthas): Waters that Remember

No temple in Kanchipuram is complete without its **tirtha**—a sacred tank, often vast, bordered by steps and stories. These waters are not ornamental; they are elemental, sanctified through time and myth. Pilgrims bathe here not to cleanse the body, but to unburden the soul.

Each tank has a name, a legend, and a rhythm:

- The **Anaikatta Kulam** near Ekambareswarar is said to have been created by Shiva himself.

- The **Pushkarni** of Varadaraja Temple hides the wooden idol of **Atthi Varadar**, submerged for decades before his resurrection in ritual.

- The **Chakra Tirtha**, associated with Vishnu's discus, is believed to be a site of absolution.

At dawn, the tanks mirror the sky; at twilight, they hold shadows of spires. They are the reflecting pools of the soul—where gods appear not in form, but in ripple and reflection.

Prakara and Circumambulation: Sacred Geometry in Motion

The **prakara**, or enclosed pathway around the sanctum, is where the devotee walks in slow, measured steps. This act of **pradakshina**—circumambulation—is not merely physical but symbolic: a walking meditation that enacts the orbit of the self around the divine center.

Many temples in Kanchipuram have multiple *prakaras*, encircling the deity like cosmic shells. The inner walls are often lined with bronze processional icons (*utsava murthis*), stories in bas-relief, and niches that house guardian deities and saints. Moving from outer prakara to inner sanctum is thus both a spatial and spiritual contraction—a journey inward.

The Temple as Cosmos, the Devotee as Pilgrim-Star

In sum, the architectural features of Kanchipuram's temples are not simply feats of engineering, but articulations of a worldview. They embody a metaphysical cartography where every stone is placed with purpose, every dimension echoes scriptural proportions, and every angle is an invitation to inner alignment.

In this sacred city, architecture is not inert. It breathes, listens, instructs. A gopuram rises like a question, a vimana resolves like a mantra. A mandapa receives the world, a tirtha returns it purified. And in the heart of it all, in the sanctum dimly lit, sits the formless made form—awaiting the devotee whose journey through light and shadow ends not in sight, but in silence.

Ritual and Festival: The Pulse of the Sacred City

If architecture is the body of Kanchipuram's sacredness, **ritual** is its breath, and **festival** is its pulse.

Within the cool stone sanctuaries and beneath the towering *gopurams*, a great choreography unfolds—daily, seasonally, eternally—linking sky and soil, gods and humans, light and time. These rituals are not performed *for* the gods but *with* them. In Kanchipuram, divinity is not distant—it dwells, eats, bathes, sleeps, travels, and rejoices with its people.

Nitya Pujas: The Rhythm of a Divine Day

Every day in a Kanchipuram temple is a microcosm of cosmic order. The daily **nitya pujas**—ritual offerings performed at prescribed times—mark the passage of sacred time, dividing the mundane day into luminous intervals.

- At **dawn**, the **Suprabhatam** is sung: gentle verses to awaken the deity, much like one would stir a beloved from sleep.

- In the **morning, Abhishekam** (ritual bathing) is performed with milk, sandalwood paste, honey, and holy water—purifying the idol not merely in act, but in symbol.
- At **noon**, food offerings (*naivedya*) are made—rice, fruits, sweet dishes—prepared with devotion and placed before the deity, who is treated not as stone but as sovereign guests.
- In the **evening**, lamps are lit, bells are rung, incense swirls upward—and the deity is ceremonially "put to rest" with lullabies and the drawing of curtains across the sanctum.

This rhythm continues regardless of season, for a time in Kanchipuram temples is **ritualized time**—circular, not linear; sacred, not secular.

Utsavams: The Journey of the Divine

Beyond the daily liturgies, each temple celebrates **Utsavams**—grand festivals where the deity is taken beyond the inner sanctum, clothed in gold and silk, and carried among the people. These festivals are **not just celebrations**—they are sacred dramas, theological enactments, and cosmic renewals.

One of the most celebrated is the **Brahmotsavam**, a multi-day pageant in which the deity's processional form (*utsava murthi*) is taken in a grand procession on elaborate vahanas (vehicles), each symbolizing a cosmic principle:

- **Garuda Vahana** - the eagle mount of Vishnu, symbolizing speed and devotion.
- **Yali Vahana** - a mythic lion-elephant hybrid, evoking strength and divine mystery.

- **Ratha (Chariot)** - the great temple car, drawn by thousands, moving like a mountain across the city, its wheels echoing the wheel of dharma.

The streets of Kanchipuram bloom with festivity—*kolams* on thresholds, lamps in doorways, and chants in every air. The god is no longer inside stone, but among flesh—blessing, beholding, being.

Atthi Varadar: The Secret God of Time

Perhaps the most mystical festival in Kanchipuram is the **Atthi Varadar Darshan**, a rare event that occurs once every **40 years** at the **Varadaraja Perumal Temple**. A wooden idol of Vishnu, carved from the sacred Atthi (fig) tree, is kept submerged in the temple tank for decades, encased in slumber beneath water and silence.

When the time arrives, the idol is lifted, anointed, and unveiled for just **48 days**. Devotees pour into the city in lakhs, lining up to glimpse the god who disappears again into the watery depths until the next cycle.

This is not a mere spectacle; it is a cosmic allegory. **The divine hides and reveals. It rests and rises.** In this festival, time becomes sacred drama, and the heart of Kanchipuram beats with timeless intensity.

Deepavali and Navaratri: Seasons of Light and Shakti

During **Navaratri**, the city turns into a gallery of goddesses. At **Kamakshi Amman Temple**, nine nights of worship unfold, culminating in the victory of light over shadow, knowledge over ignorance, and the goddess over the demon within.

In **Deepavali**, homes and temples alike gleam with earthen lamps. Processions of gods with fire-lit torches cut across the night, re-enacting the triumph of dharma.

Every festival in Kanchipuram is thus **cosmological theatre**—a re-enactment of the myths that shaped the world, re-inscribed each year to remind the community that the divine is not distant myth, but immediate presence.

Ritual as Cosmic Maintenance

Temple rituals are not superstition, nor are they mere tradition. In the worldview of Kanchipuram, **ritual maintains cosmic order**. The daily puja is a stabilizing force, the annual festival a reaffirmation of divine-human relation. When the *priest offers flame*, it is not just to the deity, but to the universe itself.

And for the devotee, participation is not passive. To walk in a festival, to chant a hymn, to offer a flower—these are acts of cosmic rebalancing. In Kanchipuram, **the ritual is not outside you; it is you**. You become the lamp, the drumbeat, the incense spiral. You become the offering and the offered.

The Eternal Festival

Thus, from the intimate murmur of a morning chant to the thunderous roar of temple chariots, the rituals and festivals of Kanchipuram transform the city into a living liturgy. Stone becomes breath. Time becomes a myth. The god who resides in stillness also walks in procession. The devotee who enters in doubt emerges with the scent of sandalwood and the glow of light glimpsed through shadow.

In Kanchipuram, every day is a rehearsal of eternity.

CHAPTER 4:

ART AND ARCHITECTURE: WHERE STONE BECOMES SCRIPTURE

In Kanchipuram, architecture is not mute masonry—it is theology made visible, art shaped by devotion, and geometry sanctified by myth. The city rises not merely in buildings, but in **visions etched into granite and sandstone**, in **pillars that pulse with motion**, and in **walls that carry the murmur of centuries**. Here, art is neither ornamental nor optional—it is integral to the spiritual experience, guiding the eye, the mind, and the soul toward the eternal.

Pallava Precision: The Birth of Sacred Stonework

The architectural soul of Kanchipuram begins with the **Pallavas** (6th to 9th centuries CE), who pioneered rock-cut and structural temples in Tamilakam. Under rulers like **Mahendravarman I** and **Narasimhavarman II (Rajasimha)**, temple design moved from cave to monument, from rudimentary to refined.

The **Kailasanathar Temple**, commissioned by Rajasimha, stands as a masterwork of early Dravidian architecture. Its *sandstone walls,* richly carved with over **240 niches**, hold miniatures of Shiva in myriad forms—**the dancer, the yogi, the slayer of ignorance**. Its layout embodies **Shiva's abode, Mount Kailasa,** rendered in sacred geometry.

Each **sculpture is a frozen hymn**, and each frieze is a philosophical statement. The ornate *dvitala vimana* (two-storey tower) surges upward like a flame—a symbol of aspiration, ascension, and spiritual fire.

Chola Grace and Granularity

Though the Cholas were centered in Thanjavur, their presence in Kanchipuram left behind jewels of refinement. They introduced **grander scale**, **bronze iconography**, and a sense of **sculptural dynamism** that enlivened temple walls and mandapas.

Chola-era temples in the city—like parts of the **Kamakshi Amman Temple**—exhibit graceful pillars with **flowing floral motifs**, **celestial maidens**, and **narrative panels** carved with fluidity and finesse. Bronze casting, perfected under Chola patronage, endowed Kanchipuram with **processional icons** of sublime beauty—gods and goddesses not frozen in posture, but alive with movement, as if caught mid-breath.

Vijayanagara Grandeur: Rise of the Gopuram

The **Vijayanagara rulers** (14th to 17th centuries) reshaped Kanchipuram's skyline with their characteristic flair: **lofty gopurams**, **hundred-pillared mandapas**, and expansive **prakara walls**. Temples like **Varadaraja Perumal** and **Ekambareswarar** expanded into monumental complexes with **intricate ceiling carvings**, **horse-riding warriors**, **yali-striding pillars**, and **mythical tableaux**.

In these works, narrative meets monumentality. Gods are flanked by mortals; sages speak to kings; lions leap from column capitals; dancers whirl on stone brackets. The fusion of **drama, devotion, and discipline** defines this era's architectural grammar.

The **thousand-pillared hall** of Varadaraja Perumal Temple, though technically numbering in the hundreds, is a marvel of rhythm and detail: each pillar a story, each carving a chapter in stone scripture.

Sculpture: A Dance in Stone

From the leaping *Nataraja* to the serene *Dakshinamurti*, Kanchipuram's sculptural idiom captures movement and stillness alike. The **iconographic canons** of the Agamas are followed with precision, yet the artistry breathes individuality.

- **Faces of deities** are serene but not still—alive with inner joy, fierce compassion, or motherly grace.
- **Torso proportions** follow the golden ratio (*tala system*), balancing symmetry with sensuality.

- **Mudras (hand gestures)** are frozen mid-blessing or mid-dialogue—conveying entire doctrines in a flick of a finger or curl of palm.

Even **ceiling carvings**, often overlooked, are intricate mandalas—lotuses, cosmic wheels, stars—reminding the viewer to look up, always.

Temple as Total Artwork

Kanchipuram's temples are not merely sculpted structures—they are **total artworks**. Every aspect, from **the flagstaff to the floor**, participates in sacred meaning. The **outer walls** serve as protective mantras. The **inner walls** become canvases of deity and devotion. The **mandapas** are theatres of ritual, while the **vimanas** reach like mantras into the sky.

Stone and space become scripture. Architecture becomes **darsana**—a vision. For the devotee walking through Kanchipuram's temple corridors, art does not decorate religion—it *reveals* it.

Art as Illumination

In Kanchipuram, art is not separate from enlightenment—it *is* enlightenment. Every chisel stroke, every measured pillar, and every dancing form is a call to wakefulness. As light filters through temple corridors and shadows fall on carved limbs of gods, a silent teaching resounds:

Stone remembers. Space listens. The divine lives not only in heaven—but here, in the very lines and curves of sacred design.

Thus, Kanchipuram remains not just a city of temples, but a city of living art—a stone manuscript, ever open to those who walk its halls with reverence.

CHAPTER 5:

THE LOOM AND THE SACRED THREAD

The Loom and the Sacred Thread—a phrase that beautifully captures the essence of Kanchipuram's rich tradition of silk weaving—can be seen as both a celebration of craftsmanship and a deep reflection of spiritual significance.

In Kanchipuram, the silk saree is not just a piece of clothing, but a symbol of divine beauty and sacred rituals. The process of weaving these intricate textiles passed down through generations, can be seen as a form of sacred labor. Each thread in the loom holds within it a cultural and spiritual narrative, weaving together threads of history, devotion, and artistry. This sacredness stems not only from the quality of the silk itself but from the reverence with which the weavers approach their craft.

The loom, an instrument of creation, becomes a metaphor for the divine act of creation in many religious traditions. In Kanchipuram, the weaver's role is akin to a devotee performing sacred duties. The meticulous weaving process is often done in small family workshops, where the weavers take care to follow traditional patterns and methods, while also paying homage to the divine in their work. The act of weaving itself is ritualistic, and many families involve prayers and blessings before beginning a new weaving project.

The sacred thread, known as the *pattu,* is often associated with purity and divine blessing. In Hindu rituals, the sacred thread (*yajnopavita* or *janeyu*) is a symbol of spiritual awakening and the wearer's connection to divine knowledge. Similarly, the *pattu* thread in Kanchipuram silk sarees is woven with sacred intent, often in temples, and has been intertwined with various deities and religious rites. The thread in these garments transcends mere material value, representing the spiritual continuity between the weaver, the wearer, and the divine.

When brides in Tamil culture wear Kanchipuram sarees, they are not just donning a beautiful garment—they are enveloped in a spiritual tradition that binds them to a lineage of sacred artistry. The saree, often intricately designed with motifs of deities, temples, and natural elements, carries blessings and protection for the wearer. These sarees are not only symbols of beauty but of divine craftsmanship and the eternal cycle of creation and devotion.

The evolution of the Kanchipuram silk saree, while deeply rooted in tradition, reflects the dynamic interplay between craftsmanship, religion, and modern influences. Over time, the weaving techniques and motifs have evolved, adapting to changes in taste, technology, and cultural exchanges. However, the spiritual essence of the saree remains intact, woven into its threads like a timeless narrative.

The Weaving Tradition: From Sacred Craft to Artisanal Excellence

In its earliest days, the Kanchipuram silk weaving tradition was primarily a religious craft, often performed by families in temple towns, with the blessings of the deities. These weavers were seen as artisans of devotion, creating garments for priests, temple rituals, and royal patrons. The loom was treated as a sacred space, where every thread was meticulously woven to not only form intricate patterns but also to uphold divine aesthetics. Over the centuries, these traditions were passed down, ensuring that every generation knew the ancient techniques of weaving, dyeing, and designing.

With the advent of industrialization and modern textile technologies, the way Kanchipuram sarees were produced began to shift. The introduction of mechanized looms and synthetic dyes posed challenges to traditional handloom techniques. Yet, Kanchipuram weavers managed to adapt by using modern tools while still adhering to the age-old traditions of hand-weaving, making sure that the saree retained its aura of sacredness. Today, while the craft of weaving remains largely handloom-based, advancements in the process have allowed for greater speed and precision, ensuring that these revered garments continue to be woven with the same care and attention to detail as in the past.

Evolution of Motifs and Design

The design motifs on Kanchipuram sarees have also evolved, reflecting a broader cultural shift. Traditionally, these sarees featured motifs inspired by Hindu iconography—gods and goddesses, temples, lotus flowers, and intricate geometric patterns. Each design had a symbolic meaning, often believed to bring prosperity, health, and blessings to the wearer.

In the modern era, the influence of globalization, travel, and multiculturalism has led to the incorporation of newer motifs. Contemporary Kanchipuram sarees may feature Western-inspired designs, such as floral patterns, abstract art, or even the infusion of metallic threads. However, the core of the designs—the themes of divine grace, auspiciousness, and beauty—has remained unchanged. What once was sacred symbolism is now a more diverse fusion of cultures, where traditional motifs coexist with new-age interpretations.

From Rituals to Fashion: The Modern Kanchipuram Saree

Today, the Kanchipuram silk saree is no longer limited to religious ceremonies or royal events. It has seamlessly made its way into the realm of fashion, worn by women across the world for weddings, festivals, and formal occasions. While the sacred thread and the spiritual association remain a part of the saree's identity, its place in contemporary fashion reflects how tradition can coexist with modernity.

For instance, many modern brides, while still honoring the traditional practice of wearing Kanchipuram sarees during their weddings, now pair them with contemporary accessories and experiment with fashion-forward styles. Celebrity endorsements, social media influencers, and the rise of online shopping have made these sarees accessible to a global audience, enhancing their prestige and demand. This shift from a purely ritualistic garment to an object of luxury and fashion demonstrates the versatility of the Kanchipuram saree in the modern world.

Cultural and Religious Significance in the Modern Context

Despite the shifts in design and usage, the spiritual connection between the weaver, the garment, and the wearer continues to be emphasized. Many families still visit temples to seek blessings before starting a new weaving project, and many brides still honor the sacredness of the Kanchipuram saree by incorporating it into their wedding ceremonies. The notion of the *pattu*—the sacred thread that connects the weaver's work to divine blessings—remains a key feature of these garments, making them not just a symbol of beauty, but a conduit for protection, auspiciousness, and prosperity.

Even in contemporary times, the process of weaving and wearing a Kanchipuram saree is a statement of cultural pride, one that connects wearers to their heritage. The skill and devotion of the weavers, the intricate craftsmanship of the saree, and its deep-rooted cultural significance are all preserved in the fabric, ensuring that each new generation continues to honor the past while embracing the present.

The Loom's Future: Sustainability and Innovation

As the world grows more conscious of sustainability, there is a renewed focus on preserving traditional crafts like the Kanchipuram silk weaving tradition. Ethical fashion movements are now championing the sustainability of handloom weaving, which uses natural dyes, and sustainable practices, and promotes fair trade. The slow fashion movement has given Kanchipuram sarees a new place in the market, where their timeless beauty and environmental benefits are appreciated.

The future of the Kanchipuram silk saree lies in maintaining a delicate balance between honoring its sacred past and embracing the opportunities of the modern world. Innovations in design, marketing, and sustainability will ensure that these sacred threads continue to weave the tapestry of culture, beauty, and spirituality for generations to come.

The source of the silk used in Kanchipuram sarees is as integral to their identity as the weaving process itself. The quality, texture, and sheen of Kanchipuram silk have earned it a place of reverence, not only in the world of fashion but also in cultural and religious rituals. The silk used in these sarees is typically derived from *Bombyx mori*—the silkworm known for producing the finest silk threads.

The Silkworm and Its Sacred Connection

The silk thread begins its journey in the cocoon of the silkworm, which is a creature deeply embedded in the mythological and cultural narratives of India. In the context of Kanchipuram silk weaving, the process of rearing and harvesting the silkworms, followed by the extraction of the silk fibers, is a meticulous practice that involves both natural and spiritual care.

In the traditional weaving communities around Kanchipuram, the process of obtaining silk is often carried out with reverence. The silkworms are bred in controlled environments, where they are fed mulberry leaves, which are essential for the production of high-quality silk. The silkworms spin their cocoons over a period of several days, which are later harvested. This method of production—entirely organic and reliant on the delicate life cycle of the silkworm—reflects a spiritual bond between nature, the artisan, and the fabric that is to be created.

The *Bombyx mori* silkworm produces long, smooth fibers that are prized for their strength and luster. These fibers, once harvested, are unwound from the cocoon in a delicate process known as *reeling*. The length and smoothness of the silk fibers are key factors in producing the characteristic richness of Kanchipuram silk. The silks are typically reeled in the natural, un-dyed state before being dyed using traditional methods.

Mulberry Silk: The Heart of Kanchipuram Sarees

The majority of the silk used for Kanchipuram sarees comes from *mulberry* trees, with *Bombyx mori* silkworms feeding on the leaves. This type of silk is particularly valued for its superior texture and durability. Unlike other types of silk, which might be obtained from various sources such as wild silkworms (*tussar* silk), mulberry silk has a smooth, fine texture that allows the intricate designs and vibrant colors of the Kanchipuram sarees to shine.

The mulberry-fed silkworm produces silk that has a unique sheen, often described as a glowing or radiant quality. This lustrous characteristic is one of the reasons Kanchipuram silk sarees are so revered. The durability and resilience of mulberry silk also allow the sarees to maintain their rich sheen over time, even after frequent wear, which makes them a prized possession passed down through generations.

Natural Dyeing and the Spiritual Significance

In traditional Kanchipuram silk weaving, the dyeing process is as important as the weaving itself. Natural dyes, derived from plants, minerals, and other organic sources, were historically used to color silk. This method of dyeing ensured that the colors would be rich and vibrant, yet environmentally friendly.

Many of the dyes used in Kanchipuram silk are symbolic. For instance, *kumkum* (a red pigment made from turmeric and other natural sources) is often used to dye silk in sacred hues of red, symbolizing strength, vitality, and auspiciousness. Gold and silver threads, often woven into the saree's borders or designs, represent purity, divinity, and royalty. These metallic threads are typically made of real gold or silver, which is painstakingly coated onto the silk threads, giving the saree an added dimension of luxury and sacredness.

The sacredness of the silk is often invoked during the dyeing process, as the weavers and dyers offer prayers or seek blessings for the success of the product. This ensures that each saree, even before it is woven, is imbued with a sense of spiritual intent and purity.

Sustainability and Ethical Practices

The silk trade in Kanchipuram has long been rooted in sustainable practices. Mulberry silk production, which is at the heart of Kanchipuram's legacy, has a relatively minimal environmental impact when compared to industrial textile production. The weavers, often part of tight-knit, family-run operations, maintain traditional practices passed down for centuries, which focus on long-term sustainability rather than mass production.

However, in recent years, there has been a growing movement within the industry to embrace even more sustainable practices. These include innovations in silk farming that are less harmful to the environment, as well as efforts to preserve biodiversity by ensuring the silkworms' natural habitat is maintained. Moreover, some modern Kanchipuram saree producers have begun experimenting with plant-based dyes, eco-friendly silks, and organic mulberry farming, creating a more sustainable and ethical product for the future.

Kanchipuram Silk in the Global Market

The increasing demand for Kanchipuram silk has led to its spread beyond traditional borders. While it remains a symbol of Indian heritage, the allure of Kanchipuram sarees has captured the attention of fashion enthusiasts and collectors worldwide. The silk's unparalleled quality and rich history make it a desirable item for connoisseurs of fine textiles. The process from silkworm to finished saree is now marketed as a high-end luxury, often accompanied by stories about the silk's origins and the sacredness embedded in its creation.

The global demand for Kanchipuram silk also means that the artisans are increasingly aware of the need to balance tradition with the modern market. Innovations in both design and production have helped maintain the relevance of Kanchipuram silk in a fast-paced, fashion-forward world while still respecting its cultural roots.

The Sacred Thread: From Silk to Spirit

In the context of Kanchipuram sarees, the silk thread is not merely a material but a bridge between the earthly and the divine. The silkworm, the mulberry leaves, the dyeing process, and the intricate weaving all come together to create a fabric that is more than just a garment. It is a sacred object, a piece of heritage, and a symbol of continuity between past and future generations. The silk itself, sourced from nature and shaped by human hands, carries the essence of both tradition and devotion, offering the wearer a deep connection to the divine.

CHAPTER 6:

FESTIVALS AND RITUAL LIFE THE ROLE OF KANCHIPURAM SILK IN RELIGIOUS FESTIVALS

The connection between Kanchipuram silk and festivals can be seen in the elaborate celebrations that take place throughout the year, especially at the famed temples of Kanchipuram. These festivals are marked by grand processions, rituals, and celebrations that honor the deities residing in the temples.

Pongal Festival:

One of the most significant festivals in Tamil Nadu, including Kanchipuram, is Pongal, a harvest festival that celebrates the bounty of the land. During this festival, families offer prayers to the Sun God, cattle, and farm tools, acknowledging the earth's fertility. It is also a time for renewing connections to community and tradition. On this day, women often wear new Kanchipuram sarees, symbolizing prosperity and divine favor. The sarees, rich in colors and patterns, are seen as an offering of gratitude and respect to the gods.

Vaikunta Ekadasi:

In Kanchipuram, this festival is dedicated to Lord Vishnu and is observed with great reverence. The Vaikunta Ekadasi is considered one of the holiest days for devotees, and the temples of Kanchipuram, including the renowned *Varadaraja Perumal Temple*, are beautifully adorned with flowers and lights. Devotees, particularly women, wear Kanchipuram silk sarees during temple visits to mark the occasion. The saree, with its spiritual connection, is considered an offering to the deity, signifying the devotee's respect and reverence.

Shivaratri:

Another major festival in Kanchipuram, dedicated to Lord Shiva, is *Mahashivaratri*. This festival involves night-long prayers, fasting, and temple worship. As with other sacred events, women often choose to wear Kanchipuram silk sarees during temple visits and rituals. The ritual significance of wearing these sarees goes beyond fashion; it represents the devotee's spiritual purity and commitment. The saree is thought to be a conduit for divine blessings, an earthly garment that connects the wearer to the sacred.

Ritual Significance of the Saree in Temples

In Kanchipuram, silk sarees also play a prominent role in temple rituals. The process of dedicating a saree to a deity in the temple is an act of reverence, where the saree is offered as a *prasadam* (blessed offering). The significance of this offering is deeply embedded in the ritual life of the region, where the devotion of the people is reflected in the sacred garment.

Temple Processions:

During temple festivals, deities are carried in grand processions, often wearing beautiful silk garments. The divine statues are dressed in Kanchipuram silk sarees, and these sarees are treated with the utmost reverence. It is not unusual for devotees to donate expensive silk sarees to the temple as part of their devotion. These donations are seen as a means of ensuring blessings, prosperity, and divine favor.

Bride's Saree as a Ritual Offering:

In the context of marriage, the Kanchipuram silk saree holds ritual importance as well. The bride, draped in her Kanchipuram silk saree, often wears it during temple visits, where it is blessed by the priest before the wedding ceremony. The saree is not just a garment for the wedding day; it is also a symbol of the bride's connection to her heritage, family, and spiritual lineage. The silk threads of the saree are seen as carrying blessings and positive energy that will protect the bride and guide her in her married life.

Sacred Textiles in Ritual Offerings

The sacredness of the Kanchipuram silk saree extends beyond the individual wearer to include communal and temple-related offerings. The silk saree is often used in rituals as an offering to the gods in exchange for divine protection, prosperity, or blessings for the family. In some temples, the offering of a silk saree is a form of *votive offering*, where the devotee seeks to fulfill a wish or express gratitude for blessings received.

For example, in Kanchipuram, the famed *Ekambareswarar Temple* dedicated to Lord Shiva, devotees may present a Kanchipuram silk saree as part of their prayer. The act of gifting the saree is done with the belief that the deity will bless them with success, health, and happiness. After the ritual, the temple may use the saree to dress the deity or in some cases, give it to the temple's priests or the community as a symbol of sacred exchange.

The Sacred Thread of Devotion

Beyond its aesthetic appeal, the Kanchipuram silk saree carries deep religious and spiritual symbolism. The threads, carefully spun from silk, represent the *samskaras* (rituals) that bind the individual to the divine. In Hindu tradition, the idea of thread plays a critical role in the performance of sacred rituals. The sacred thread (*yajnopavita*) worn by male priests and others in the community symbolizes their connection to divine knowledge and spirituality. Similarly, the silk thread of the saree, woven with devotion and care, connects the wearer to a higher realm, embodying sacredness, purity, and grace.

In rituals such as the *kanyadaan* (giving away of the bride) during marriage, the bride is dressed in a Kanchipuram saree, signifying her purity and her connection to the divine as she transitions into married life. This act mirrors the giving of the sacred thread in other rites, a powerful and spiritual gesture linking the individual to both tradition and the divine.

Festivals as Cultural Expressions of Devotion

Festivals in Kanchipuram are not just religious observances; they are expressions of the culture, heritage, and community life that bind the people together. The wearing of Kanchipuram silk sarees during these festivals serves as a visual representation of this unity. The saree, with its deep connection to both divine worship and cultural continuity, becomes a living testament to the heritage of Kanchipuram, a sacred thread that ties the present generation to their ancestors and their faith.

Kanchipuram's festivals, with their vibrant processions, temple rituals, and community celebrations, are a living tapestry woven together by devotion, tradition, and the sacredness of the Kanchipuram silk saree. These garments transcend the role of simple attire, becoming sacred symbols of divine protection, cultural pride, and the timeless connection between humanity and the divine.

CHAPTER 7:

KANCHIPURAM: A HISTORICAL CENTER FOR PHILOSOPHICAL THOUGHT

Kanchipuram's reputation as a center for learning is rooted in its history, which stretches back to the Pallava dynasty and earlier. Under the rule of the Pallavas, Kanchipuram became a prominent center of art, culture, and intellectual pursuits. The Pallavas, great patrons of art and philosophy, supported the establishment of numerous learning institutions, particularly those focused on religious and philosophical studies.

During this period, Kanchipuram became the seat of several important philosophical traditions, most notably the Vedantic schools of thought. The city has been associated with the development of the *Advaita Vedanta* philosophy, which emphasizes the oneness of the individual soul (*atman*) with the universal soul (*Brahman*). The teachings of Adi Shankaracharya, one of the most influential philosophers in Indian history, were instrumental in shaping the intellectual landscape of Kanchipuram. Shankaracharya is believed to have visited the city and had a lasting impact on the religious and philosophical traditions that flourished there.

The Role of Temples as Centers of Learning

The temples of Kanchipuram were not just places of worship; they were also hubs of learning. Many of the grand temples, such as the *Kailasanathar Temple, Varadaraja Perumal Temple,* and *Ekambareswarar Temple,* served as centers for intellectual engagement. Scholars, poets, and philosophers gathered in these temples to engage in discussions on religious texts, philosophy, and spirituality.

In the *Vedanta* tradition, the temples played a pivotal role in the study and dissemination of sacred texts such as the *Upanishads, Bhagavad Gita,* and the *Brahma Sutras.* Temples were also the sites of *pancharatra* rituals and other esoteric practices, which involved a deep understanding of philosophical concepts. The priests and scholars who resided in these temples were not only custodians of the rituals but also teachers and mentors in the fields of Vedanta, Tamil literature, and sacred knowledge.

Philosophical Schools and Scholars of Kanchipuram

Kanchipuram was home to several renowned scholars who contributed to the philosophical discourse in India. The city became a critical intellectual center, especially during the early medieval period.

The Philosophical Influence of Adi Shankaracharya

One of the most significant figures associated with Kanchipuram's intellectual heritage is Adi Shankaracharya. Although his spiritual journey took him across the subcontinent, Shankaracharya's visit to Kanchipuram marked a significant moment in the intellectual history of the city. He is believed to have established one of the four *mathas*(monastic orders) in Kanchipuram, which became instrumental in spreading the philosophy of *Advaita Vedanta*.

Through his teachings, Shankaracharya emphasized the non-dual nature of existence, arguing that the ultimate reality (*Brahman*) is beyond all distinctions, and the individual self (*atman*) is one with this supreme reality. His influence can still be seen today in Kanchipuram's continued tradition of Vedantic scholarship.

Ramanuja and Vishishtadvaita Vedanta

In addition to Shankaracharya, another towering figure in Kanchipuram's philosophical legacy is Ramanuja, the proponent of *Vishishtadvaita Vedanta* (qualified non-dualism). Ramanuja, who was born in the nearby village of Sriperumbudur, spent much of his life in Kanchipuram, where he studied, taught, and debated the intricacies of Vedantic philosophy. He argued that while Brahman is the ultimate reality, the individual soul retains its identity and is eternally connected to Brahman through devotion.

Ramanuja's teachings revolutionized the understanding of devotion (*bhakti*) in the context of Vedanta. His interpretation emphasized the importance of surrendering to the divine will and devotion to God as a means of realizing spiritual liberation. Ramanuja's influence is deeply embedded in the spiritual practices of Kanchipuram, where temples dedicated to Vishnu continue to serve as centers of devotion and philosophy.

The Alvars and Nayanmars: Tamil Bhakti Poetry

Kanchipuram has also been central to the *Bhakti movement,* a devotional movement that sought to bridge the divide between the individual and the divine through direct, personal devotion. The *Alvars* (devotees of Vishnu) and *Nayanmars* (devotees of Shiva) were key figures in this movement, and their devotional hymns—composed in Tamil—played a significant role in shaping the religious and philosophical landscape of Kanchipuram.

The Alvars' *Tiruvaymoli* (sacred utterances) and the Nayanmars' *Tevaram* (sacred hymns) are foundational texts in Tamil literature, and their teachings on devotion and philosophy have influenced generations of thinkers in Kanchipuram. These hymns, which emphasize the power of divine grace and love, are still sung in temples during daily rituals and festivals, keeping the philosophical and spiritual traditions alive.

Kanchipuram's Role in Tamil Literature

In addition to its association with Vedanta and the Bhakti movement, Kanchipuram has also contributed significantly to the development of Tamil literature. As a seat of learning, the city has produced some of the most influential Tamil poets, scholars, and philosophers.

The Sangam Age and Early Philosophical Texts

During the *Sangam* period (circa 300 BCE to 300 CE), Kanchipuram was a significant cultural center where early Tamil poetic works were composed. These poems, often reflecting the themes of ethics, politics, and philosophy, laid the foundation for the Tamil philosophical tradition. The *Tolkappiyam,* the earliest known treatise on Tamil grammar, was likely composed in or influenced by the intellectual climate of cities like Kanchipuram.

The Influence of Tamil Shaivism

The Tamil Shaivite tradition, which flourished in Kanchipuram, also contributed to the intellectual environment of the region. Philosophers like *Meykandar,* who was instrumental in the development of *Shaiva Siddhanta* philosophy, called Kanchipuram home. Shaiva Siddhanta, a system of philosophy that emphasized the worship of Lord Shiva as the supreme reality, was an influential school of thought that shaped both the religious and philosophical discourse in Kanchipuram.

The Modern Revival of Kanchipuram's Philosophical Legacy

In contemporary times, Kanchipuram continues to be a hub for philosophical study and spiritual inquiry. Scholars and spiritual seekers from around the world visit Kanchipuram to explore its rich philosophical heritage. The city's temples, now UNESCO World Heritage Sites, attract pilgrims and tourists alike, eager to witness the fusion of devotion and intellectual rigor.

The *Sri Sankaracharya University of Traditional Studies* and other educational institutions in Kanchipuram offer programs focused on philosophy, theology, and Sanskrit studies, preserving the city's reputation as a center for learning. These institutions help keep alive the teachings of Shankaracharya, Ramanuja, and other great thinkers, ensuring that the philosophical traditions of Kanchipuram remain relevant in the modern age.

CONCLUSION:

KANCHIPURAM AS A LIVING SEAT OF LEARNING

Kanchipuram's legacy as a seat of learning and philosophy is profound and enduring. From the teachings of Shankaracharya and Ramanuja to the devotional poetry of the Alvars and Nayanmars, the city has played a pivotal role in shaping the intellectual and spiritual landscape of India. Its temples, monasteries, and educational institutions continue to foster an environment of inquiry, devotion, and philosophical exploration, ensuring that Kanchipuram remains a living repository of knowledge and spiritual wisdom.

GLOSSARY

- **Divya Desam**: One of the 108 sacred Vishnu temples mentioned in Tamil Vaishnava tradition.
- **Gopuram**: Monumental tower at the entrance of a temple, often richly decorated.
- **Mandapam**: A pillared hall within a temple used for rituals and gatherings.
- **Pancha Bhoota Sthalam**: Five temples representing the five elements (earth, water, fire, air, ether).

- **Vimana**: The tower above the sanctum sanctorum of a temple.
- **Zari**: Metallic thread traditionally made of gold or silver, used in weaving silk sarees.
- **Yali**: Mythical lion-like creature used in temple and textile motifs.
- **Agama**: Scriptures outlining temple construction, rituals, and theology.
- **Pathshala**: Traditional school for religious and scriptural learning.